George Washington

A Buddy Book
by
Christy DeVillier

ABDO
Publishing Company

VISIT US AT

www.abdopub.com

Published by ABDO Publishing Company, 4940 Viking Drive, Edina, Minnesota 55435.
Copyright © 2001 by Abdo Consulting Group, Inc. International copyrights reserved in all
countries. No part of this book may be reproduced in any form without written permission
from the publisher.

Printed in the United States.

Edited by: Michael P. Goecke
Contributing Editor: Matt Ray
Image Research: Deborah Coldiron, Susan Will
Graphic Design: Jane Halbert
Cover Photograph: courtesy of Library of Congress, Washington, D.C.
Interior Photographs/Illustrations: pages 4, 12, 17, 18 & 19: courtesy of Library of Congress,
Washington, D.C.; pages 5, 10, 13, 15, 16, 20 & 23: courtesy of Mount Vernon Ladies
Association, Mount Vernon, VA

Library of Congress Cataloging-in-Publication Data

Devillier, Christy, 1971-
    George Washington / Christy Devillier.
      p. cm. — (First biographies)
    Includes index.
    ISBN 1-57765-593-1
    1. Washington, George, 1732-1799—Juvenile literature. 2. Presidents—United
    States—Biography—Juvenile literature. [1. Washington, George, 1732-1799. 2.
    Presidents.] I. Title.

E312.66 .D48 2001
973.4'1'092--dc21
[B]
                                                            2001022021

Table Of Contents

Why Is He Famous?

George Washington

We know George Washington as "The Father of Our Country." He was the first president of the United States. The United States president is in charge of the country.

George Washington was an excellent army leader. He led the army in the American Revolutionary War. He won many battles against the British. With his help, Americans won independence from Great Britain.

George Washington helped America win independence.

Washington's Family

George Washington was born in 1732. He grew up in Westmoreland County. This county was in Virginia. In 1738, George's family moved to Ferry Farm. George's father, Augustine, grew tobacco there.

The United States of America

Virginia →

Young George played with his brothers and sisters. George dreamed of sailing on a British warship one day. Yet, his mother, Mary, told him he could never go to sea. She knew that the British did not treat Americans fairly.

Growing Up

When George Washington was only 11 years old, his father died. George's older brother, Lawrence, was like a father to young George. Lawrence showed him how to hunt and fish.

George enjoyed visiting Lawrence at Mount Vernon. Mount Vernon was a farm. This farm was near the Potomac River in Virginia.

A Surveyor measures land.

When George was 16, he helped survey new land. Surveying means measuring the land. This land was on Virginia's western frontier. He learned a lot about living in the wild. He enjoyed the natural beauty of Virginia.

First Steps

George Washington got a job as a surveyor when he was 17. They paid him very well. George saved his money and bought land.

In 1752, Lawrence died of tuberculosis. George moved into Mount Vernon.

Mount Vernon

Later, George Washington decided to join the Virginia militia. The militia helps the army in times of need. The Virginia militia helped the British army guard America's western frontier.

George was an officer in the Virginia militia. He fought in the French and Indian War. This was a war between Great Britain and France.

After the war, George moved back to Mount Vernon. He married Martha Custis. Martha Custis's first husband had died. They had two children. These children were John and Martha. George helped Martha raise her children.

Martha, George, and family.

George and Martha owned many slaves. They helped George with his farm. They planted tobacco, wheat, oats, peaches, and apples at Mount Vernon. These slaves did not have to work after Martha Custis died. George let them go. He gave these slaves their independence.

George had a farm.

The American Revolution

In the early 1770's, Great Britain still ruled America. Slowly, Americans became angry with Great Britain. The Americans did not like some of Britain's laws. The Americans were tired of paying high taxes to Great Britain. In 1774, Americans decided to fight for independence.

Washington trained an army to fight the British.

The Americans needed an army to fight the British. They needed a leader for this army, too. They picked George Washington. Washington wanted to help America win independence. So, he agreed to lead Americans into battle.

The Continental Army

George Washington was the commander in chief, or leader, of the Continental Army. This Continental Army was made up of American soldiers and militia men.

George Washington in his army uniform.

Washington led the Continental Army.

The militia men were normal working people. They were farmers and storekeepers. Most of these men were not trained as soldiers. They did not have army uniforms, either.

The Continental
Army used cannons.

Battling The British

Washington was a skilled army leader.

George Washington directed the Continental Army very well. He surprised the British army several times in battle. Sometimes, he stopped the British from getting war supplies, too.

The Americans fought well in the beginning of the American Revolutionary War. On March 17, 1776, Washington and his army pushed the British out of Boston. This was an important win for the Americans.

George Washington won many battles.

Later, America stated that it was an independent, or free, nation. American leaders signed the Declaration of Independence on July 4th, 1776. This did not mean that the war was over, though.

Washington and the Continental Army suffered many losses. The British army was big and powerful. By 1777, the Continental Army did not have enough supplies to attack the British.

Winning The War

The Americans needed help to win the American Revolutionary War. France agreed to help America fight the British.

On October 19, 1781, the British surrendered to George Washington in Yorktown, Virginia. The American Revolutionary War was finally over. Great Britain and America signed a peace treaty on November 25, 1781.

George Washington and his family.

On December 19, 1783, George Washington left the Continental Army. He went back to his family at Mount Vernon.

The First President

In 1757, many American leaders met in Philadelphia, Pennsylvania. They talked about a new Constitution for the United States. Also, they decided that the United States needed a president. They chose George Washington. On April 30, 1789, Washington became the first United States president. He was 57 years old.

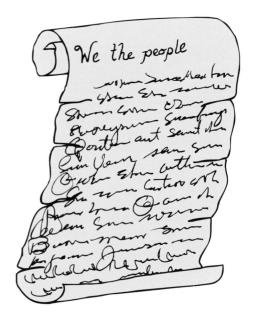

George Washington was a very good president. He knew the problems that the United States faced. He knew the important leaders of each state.

After serving another term, George Washington retired to Mount Vernon.

On December 14, 1799, George Washington died. He was 67 years old.

An American Hero

Do you know what George Washington looks like? Have you seen his face on:

- American one-dollar bills?
- American quarters (coins)?
- Mount Rushmore?

Can you find George Washington's face on Mount Rushmore?

There is a very famous tribute to George Washington. It is the Washington Monument. This monument is in Washington, D.C. Washington, D.C. is the United States capital. Why do you think we call it Washington, D.C.? It is named after George Washington, of course!

All these things remind us of George Washington. They remind us of everything he did to help the United States of America.

The Washington Monument.

Important Dates

February 22, 1732 George Washington is born.

1752 George's brother, Lawrence, dies.

1774 Americans go to war with Great Britain.

March 17, 1776 George Washington's army wins the first battle against the British.

July 4, 1776 American leaders sign the Declaration of Independence.

October 19, 1781 The British surrender to George Washington. The Americans win the war!

November 25, 1781 Great Britain and the United States sign a peace treaty.

April 30, 1789 George Washington becomes the first United States president.

December 14, 1799 George Washington dies at the age of 67.

Important Words

American Revolutionary War Americans fought for freedom
from Great Britain in this famous war.

capital the city that is home to government leaders.

Constitution the basic laws of the United States.

Declaration of Independence a document that says
America is free to rule themselves.

frontier land that has not been settled by people, the wild.

independence to be free from someone or something.

slaves people who are forced to work for nothing in return.

surrender to give up.

tax money charged by a city or country.

treaty an agreement.

tribute something that honors a special person.

Web Sites

Mount Vernon Educational Resources
http://www.mountvernon.org/education
Portraits of Washington and a full biography can be found at
this great educational site.

George Washington
http://www.walika.com/sr/washbio.htm
This site provides details on Washington's career including
some of his speeches.

Index